For Albert Uderzo—J. M.

WHAT YOU NEVER KNEW ABOUT

around-the-house HISTORY

BEDS, BEDROOMS, & PAJAMAS

BY **Patricia Lauber**   ILLUSTRATED BY **John Manders**

Aladdin Paperbacks

New York   London   Toronto   Sydney

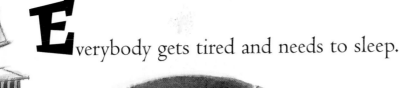

Everybody gets tired and needs to sleep.

Much of the time, horses sleep standing up.

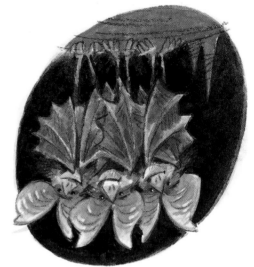

Bats sleep while hanging upside down.

Humans like to sleep lying down. In North America and Europe and other parts of the world, most people sleep in beds with frames, mattresses, sheets, blankets, and pillows. And beds are usually found in special rooms that were named for them—in bedrooms. But it wasn't always this way.

Of course, bedrooms are used for a lot of things besides sleeping. They are also places to keep clothes, do homework, play games, entertain friends, and read. But this hasn't always been so either.

Sleeping in the Stone Age

Stone Age people spent much of their time searching for food by hunting, fishing, and gathering plants. They moved with the seasons, following the food. It must have been a tiring life. What did they do for beds? How did they stay warm on a cold winter's night? No one knows for sure, but we can guess. Most likely they cut boughs from trees, spread hides or furs over them, and used more furs as blankets. For greater warmth, a whole family probably shared a bed. Perhaps friends and relatives joined them.

While you're awake, put another log on the fire.

Some Stone Age people made tents out of hides. In these tents, platforms piled with furs may have served as beds.

Sleeping in the Ancient World

About nine thousand years ago, people in some parts of the world learned how to farm. Now they no longer had to travel in order to eat. They could raise food and live in one place all year. Villages, then towns and cities, sprang up. There were houses and palaces. And in them were beds.

The Egyptians

The earliest beds we know of are Egyptian. They are about seven thousand years old.

Egypt had no forests, and trees were scarce. The first beds were made of wicker, with cords for an under-mattress. Some were used for sleeping at night. Others were used as couches or day beds.

Later, Egypt traded grain for wood and wooden beds became common.

The head of a bed was higher than the foot. A footboard kept the sleeper from sliding off. Kings and nobles had wooden frames or bedsteads. Some frames were carved with animals, flowers, and fruit, which were inlaid with gold, ivory, and mother-of-pearl.

Sometimes it's said that Egyptians used headrests to keep their hairdos neat at night. But this cannot be so. Except for the poor, everyone wore a wig—and took it off at night. Egyptians liked to shave their heads because a bald head was easier to keep clean and free of lice.

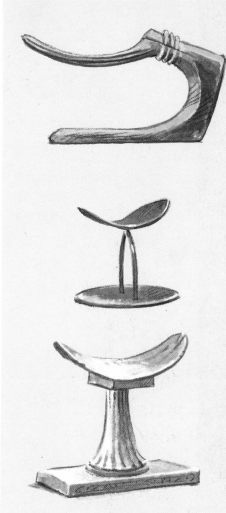

Should I wear my long hair or my braids?

Egyptians did not use pillows in bed. They used headrests, which were most often carved from wood. No one is sure why they did this, although a headrest may have been cooler than a pillow on a hot night.

The Greeks and the Romans

Like the Egyptians, the Greeks furnished their houses with day beds. So did the Romans. Wealthy people of the ancient world liked to put their feet up.

Both Greeks and Romans also had bedrooms that were more like closets than rooms. Doors were guarded at night by servants.

The Romans often read, wrote, or ate while lying down. Before lying down to dinner, they took off their shoes.

Only rich Romans had houses with day beds, bedrooms and beds, and servants. Most people were poor and lived in apartments, often one room in a shaky building without heat or piped water.

A poor person had a sack of straw for a bed, which was placed on a rough wooden platform.

Romans slept in their underwear. When going to bed, a Roman simply took off his toga and sandals. He slipped between the sheets, wearing his underpants and perhaps a tunic.

Getting up at dawn, he put his toga and sandals back on, drank a glass of water, and was ready for the day. He did not wash, because he would visit public or private baths in the afternoon.

Roman women also slept in their underwear—briefs, a linen or woolen breast-band, and perhaps a tunic. In cold weather a woman might also wear a cloak to bed.

By the year 476, attacks by barbarians had brought about the fall of Rome and its far-flung empire. When the empire crumbled, its way of life—and beds—disappeared. Europe became a patchwork of small kingdoms and states, which were often at war.

The period known today as the Middle Ages had begun. It went on for nearly a thousand years.

Sleeping in the Middle Ages

During the early Middle Ages a few people were rich. Most were poor. The rich people owned the land. The poor usually worked as peasant farmers.

The lord of the manor kept some land for himself and leased the rest to peasants. Peasants paid their rent by working the lord's land and by giving the lord part of their own harvests.

Everyone lived together under one roof—the lord of the manor and his family, servants, peasants, and sometimes livestock. Their home was a barnlike building called a "hall." It had only one room, with a hearth at its center, and was furnished with chests, benches, and long tables. In this room people cooked, ate, entertained, and slept.

They all went to bed after supper, before the fire went out. Each person was given a sack and some straw to make a bed—that is where our term "make a bed" comes from. Having made their beds, the important people laid them on the benches, tables, and chests. Everyone else slept on the floor. In the morning, beds were unmade and the straw aired out so that it would not become moldy.

The Return of the Bed and the Bedroom

There was warmth in sleeping close to others. There was also safety, for these were lawless times. Even so, some lords and ladies began to think that privacy might be nice. In time, the bedroom returned. The first bedrooms were built outside the hall, like lean-to sheds. The only way to reach them was to leave the hall and walk out through the dark and, perhaps, rain. The bedroom held only a bench and a sack of straw, but plenty of pillows, sheets, and coverlets.

By the late 1000s, at least some bedrooms had appeared indoors. There was a bedroom at one end of the great hall and above it a more private room for ladies. The rest of the hall was open.

By the late 1100s, wealthy people had bedrooms with whitewashed walls covered with tapestries. Their bedsteads were made of big timbers nailed together.

It may be damp, but at least it's mine alone!

A bedroom also held a chair, a bench, and a chest for valuables. I those days, there were no banks. Everyone thought his bedroom was the safest place to keep things of value.

During the Middle Ages, peasants and servants slept in their day clothes. The well-to-do slept naked. They wrapped themselves in a sheet before pulling the covers up, as old pictures show us. Some people did cover their heads in bed, using a kerchief worn like a turban. There is a picture from the 1200s of a lady in bed wearing only a headdress with a bunch of flowers in it. Laundry lists and household accounts first mention nightclothes in the 1500s.

In old drawings, people seem to sleep sitting up. Perhaps they did. But it's more likely that artists just drew the sleepers this way, because it is hard to show the face of a person who is lying down. We do know that kings and queens did not sleep in their crowns. Artists added the crowns to show that these people were royalty.

Sleeping Away from Home

Travel was hard. Roads were few. And in the early Middle Ages there were no inns where travelers could spend the night. The owners of manors were expected to welcome strangers.

Always room for one more! And of course you'll make a bed with us.

Much traveling was done by kings, nobles, and others who owned more than one big manor. Rents from the peasants were paid mostly in crops. The easiest way to collect them was to move the whole household from manor to manor, staying at each until the rents had been eaten up.

Late in the Middle Ages, by the 1300s, there were inns.
Travelers usually had to sleep in one big hall, several to a bed.

No one wanted to furnish several houses, so a landowner took with him his bedding and tapestries and all his furniture except the bedstead, which was too big and heavy. There would be another bedstead in the manor house he was going to.

Royal Beds

By the 1300s and 1400s, kings and queens and other nobles had very large beds. The beds often had curtains around them to make them less drafty. The king of England had layers of bedding—straw, canvas, a feather bed—which had to be smoothed with a bedstaff, and covered with sheets, blankets, and a coverlet of white fur.

In France, royal beds were so big that courtiers had to hit them with bedstaffs to make sure no one was hiding in the feathers and covers.

The Middle Ages End

From the 900s through the 1200s, many inventions changed the ways people lived and worked. Windmills sped up the grinding of grain. Horseshoes and padded horse collars made it possible to plow with horses. New seeds and new ways of planting led to bigger and better crops. A smaller number of people could produce a larger amount of food.

I'm plowing much faster with a horse.

Slow and steady is how I like it. Give me oxen any day!

Many people moved to town. Some opened shops. Earlier there had been two classes of people, the rich and the poor. Now, with the shops, a middle class was growing.

The rich lived in big manors or castles, the poor in one-room shacks. The middle class lived in houses. A house was full of people both day and night. It was a workshop or store. It was a place to do business and entertain, for there were no public places such as restaurants. It was also a place where people cooked, ate, and slept. And there were a lot of people—family, relatives, friends, servants, workers, and apprentices learning a trade. Up to twenty-five people might live and work in one big room.

A middle-class house had long tables, benches, chests, and beds. The furniture was moved around as needed. By day the tables were used for work, counting money, preparing food, and eating. At night they were taken apart and stored against the walls. Beds were unfolded and brought out. There were several beds and several people to a bed, but the beds were big, usually ten feet square.

By the mid-1400s, the Middle Ages were coming to an end. A new spirit was sweeping Europe. This was the Renaissance, a time when ideas and the arts flourished, trade grew, and explorers set out across unknown oceans. The Middle Ages had been a bridge from the ancient world to the start of the world we know.

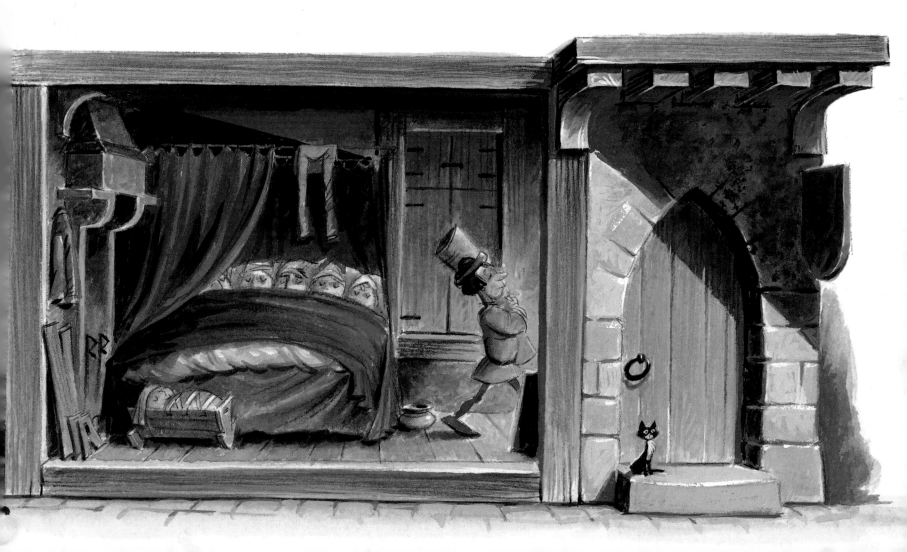

Sleeping in Changing Times

Over the next two hundred years, home life slowly changed. Houses grew bigger. Some had rooms used only for cooking. Many houses were still shops as well as places for people to live. People with money had one place for work and one for family life. The one for family life housed only family and servants. These houses gave people privacy from outsiders. But there was still very little privacy inside a house. In the early 1600s, for example, a successful architect in Paris, France, lived with his wife, seven children, and servants in two rooms. Even in big townhouses there was still not much privacy. The houses were built without hallways. One room led into another. Family, guests, and servants all passed through several rooms to get where they were going.

In the 1600s the four-poster bed became popular. It had side curtains, which kept out drafts. But it did not offer privacy, because several people slept in it.

Mama, is it morning yet?

Mama, make David stop pulling my hair.

See how neatly Sir Gawain eats off his knife? We must try to be like him.

Children Become Children

The biggest change in home life had to do with children. Once they reached the age of seven, they were sent away from home. They were expected to work and to learn from working. Even children of the upper class were sent away to noble households, where they served as pages.

In the Middle Ages, children were thought of as small grown-ups. This began to change in the 1500s. By the 1600s many middle- and upper-class children were staying at home and going to school for a few years. With children of many ages at home, families needed new sleeping arrangements.

A craftsman might have lived in a small house with his wife, eight children, two servants, and three employees. But sleepers were now divided into family and nonfamily.

Since the Middle Ages, servants had slept either in the same rooms as their masters or nearby. Now masters wanted to keep servants at a distance. In the 1700s the bell cord made this possible. When the master pulled the cord, a system of wires and pulleys rang a bell in another room and woke the servants there.

By the 1700s, big houses were divided into rooms for cooking, for dining, for entertaining, and for relaxing. Children, who were living at home, had their own bedrooms, as did other family members. Now privacy meant leaving others and going to a room of one's own. But bedrooms were not just for sleeping. They were places where children played, where wives and older girls sewed or wrote or talked quietly with a friend.

The bedroom had become the kind of room we know today. But both beds and nightclothes still had a way to go.

Great Moments in Nightclothes

In the Middle Ages, people slept naked, although most covered their heads for warmth. Around 1500, fashions changed. At night, people took off their daytime clothes and put on nightclothes. Many people have done so ever since.

1500s: Simple nightshirts were worn by men and women. Nightcaps were often red.

1600s: A man's nightshirt was as fancy as his day shirt. Little is known about what women wore.

1700s and early 1800s: Men and women wore nightshirts and nightcaps that tied under the chin.

1885: Dr. Jaeger's sleep suit reached the stores. Said to be good for the health, it was made of wool and left only the hands and face exposed to the night air.

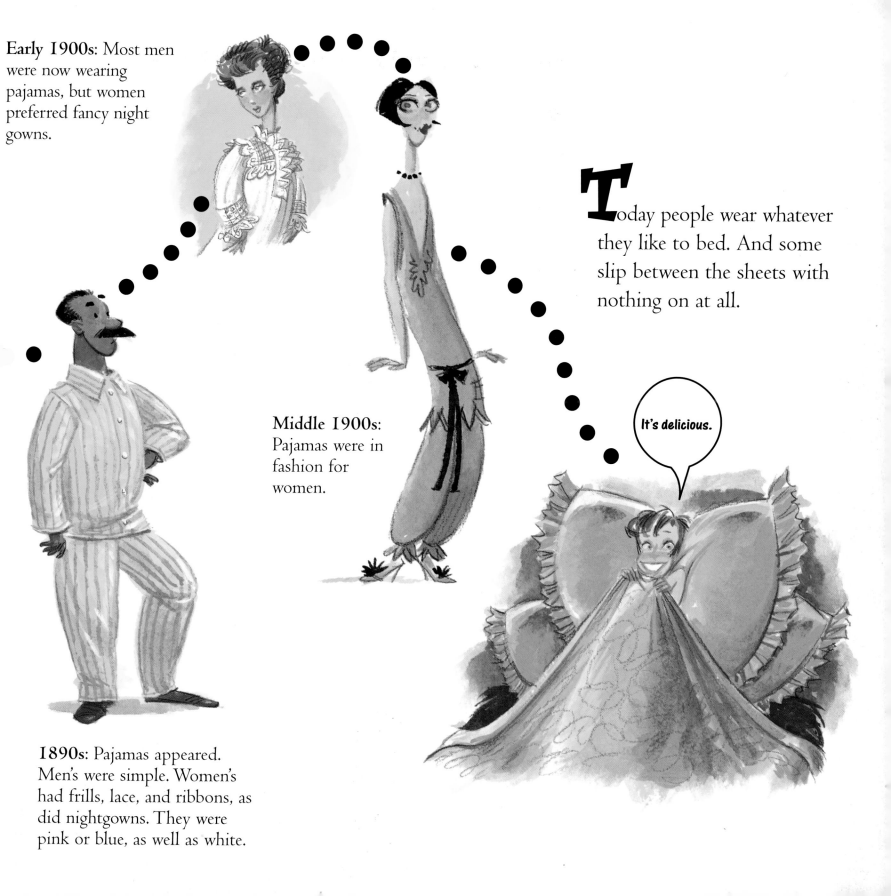

Early 1900s: Most men were now wearing pajamas, but women preferred fancy night gowns.

Today people wear whatever they like to bed. And some slip between the sheets with nothing on at all.

It's delicious.

Middle 1900s: Pajamas were in fashion for women.

1890s: Pajamas appeared. Men's were simple. Women's had frills, lace, and ribbons, as did nightgowns. They were pink or blue, as well as white.

Great Moments in Bed History

In the Middle Ages, bed frames were simple. With the passing of time they became fancier and fancier.

Plain or fancy, all beds had problems. So did sleepers, whether they were rich or poor. Anybody who went to bed was likely to be bitten—by fleas, lice, bedbugs, and other small creatures.

The biggest problem was the mattress. Its stuffing of straw, leaves, or other plant parts made a fine place for bugs to live. Unless aired and dried, it grew moldy. Sometimes mice nested in it.

Changes finally came in the late 1700s. The metal bedstead had disappeared with the fall of Rome. Now it made a comeback. Unlike wood, metal did not have cracks where bugs could hide.

Factories were built to turn out cheap cotton sheets during this time. These could be boiled when washed, without being ruined.

Also in the late 1700s, a box-shaped hair mattress replaced the sack of straw. It was clean. It didn't smell. But it was hard. Finally, in the middle 1860s, the coil-spring mattress was invented.

Springs had been invented a hundred years earlier. But they were not much used in furniture. They tended to turn over on their sides, and they broke easily. The sudden escape of a broken spring was painful.

Nothing like boiling water to get those little devils.

hey're very popular. e only have two left.

The problems were solved with better metal and the invention of springs that nested together.

At last, with the metal bedstead, cheap cotton sheets, and a coil-spring mattress, a person could sleep in comfort.

Sleeping Today

oday we usually have clean, comfortable beds both at home and when we go traveling. These beds make it easy to get a good night's sleep.

But sometimes it's fun to sleep the way people used to.

Or, if we don't want to go back to the Middle Ages and sleep on the floor, we can go back to the Stone Age and sleep on the ground.

Even when you're having fun, it's good to know that there's a comfortable bed at home for when you're tired and really need to sleep.

Bibliography

Balsdon, J. P. V. D. *Life and Leisure in Ancient Rome.* London: Phoenix Press, 2002.

Beldegreen, Alecia. *The Bed.* New York: Stewart, Tabori & Chang, 1991.

Conran, Terence. *The Bed and Bath Book.* New York: Crown Publishers, 1978.

Cunnington, C. Willet, and Phillis. *The History of Underclothes.* London: Michael Joseph, 1951.

Editors of Time-Life Books, The. *What Life Was Like in the Age of Chivalry.* Alexandria, Va.: Time-Life Books, 1997.

————*What Life Was Like on the Banks of the Nile*

————*What Life Was Like When Rome Ruled the World*

Hardyment, Christina. *Home Comfort: A History of Domestic Arrangements.* Chicago: Academy Chicago Publishers, 1992.

Heer, Friedrich. *The Medieval World.* New York: Welcome Rain, 1998.

Rybczynski, Witold. *Home: A Short History of an Idea.* New York: Viking, 1986.

Wright, Lawrence. *Warm and Snug: The History of the Bed.* London: Routledge & Kegan Paul, 1962.

Artist's Note

After spending time in the library doing research, I begin an illustration with a sketch on layout bond paper using a 2B pencil. I then trace the sketch onto Arches 300-pound hot-press watercolor paper and paint the shadow and color using a combination of Dr. Martin's dyes and Winsor & Newton watercolors. The highlights are added with Winsor & Newton Designers Gouache. Finally, I use a black Prismacolor pencil to redraw the sketch on top of the colors. This way, the fun of the sketch is preserved in the final illustration.

ALADDIN PAPERBACKS
An imprint of Simon & Schuster Children's Publishing Division
1230 Avenue of the Americas, New York, NY 10020
Text copyright © 2006 by Patricia Lauber
Illustrations copyright © 2006 by John Manders
All rights reserved, including the right of reproduction in whole or in part in any form.
ALADDIN PAPERBACKS and related logo are registered trademarks of Simon & Schuster, Inc.
Also available in a Simon and Schuster Books for Young Readers hardcover edition.
Designed by Daniel Roode
The text of this book was set in Centaur.
Manufactured in Mexico
First Aladdin Paperbacks edition January 2008
10 9 8 7 6 5 4 3 2 1
The Library of Congress has cataloged the hardcover edition as follows:
Lauber, Patricia.
What you never knew about beds, bedrooms, and pajamas / by Patricia Lauber ; illustrated by John Manders.
p. cm. — (Around the house history)
Includes bibliographical references.
1. Bedrooms. 2. Beds. 3. Pajamas. 4. Sleeping customs. I. Manders, John, ill. II. Title.
GT3000.5.B44L38 2006
392.3'6—dc22
2004020654
ISBN-13: 978-0-689-85211-4 (hc.)
ISBN-10: 0-689-85211-8 (hc.)
ISBN-13: 978-1-4169-6738-5 (pbk.)
ISBN-10: 1-4169-6738-9 (pbk.)